MAKE YOUR OWN
TOY PARACHUTE

BY CHRISTOPHER HARBO

PEBBLE
a capstone imprint

Published by Pebble, an imprint of Capstone
1710 Roe Crest Drive, North Mankato, Minnesota 56003
capstonepub.com

Copyright © 2026 by Capstone. All rights reserved. No part of this publication may be reproduced in whole or in part, or stored in a retrieval system, or transmitted in any form or by any means, electronic, mechanical, photocopying, recording, or otherwise, without written permission of the publisher.

Library of Congress Cataloging-in-Publication Data is available on the Library of Congress website.
ISBN: 9798875225260 (hardcover)
ISBN: 9798875225031 (paperback)
ISBN: 9798875225222 (ebook PDF)

Summary: Learn about physical science and gravity with this fun and easy to make science project. Gather simple supplies and follow the steps to make a parachute!

Editorial Credits
Editor: Erika L. Shores; Designer: Heidi Thompson; Media Researcher: Jo Miller; Production Specialist: Tori Abraham

Image Credits
Capstone: Karon Dubke: all project photos, supplies; Shutterstock: ANURAKE SINGTO-ON, 23, Roman023_photography, 5

The publisher and the author shall not be liable for any damages allegedly arising from the information in this book, and they specifically disclaim any liability from the use or application of any of the contents of this book.

Any additional websites and resources referenced in this book are not maintained, authorized, or sponsored by Capstone. All product and company names are trademarks™ or registered® trademarks of their respective holders.

Printed and bound in China. 6274

TABLE OF CONTENTS

Happy Landings 4

What You Need 6

What You Do 8

Take It Further 20

Behind the Science 22

Glossary 24

About the Author 24

Words in **BOLD** are in the glossary.

HAPPY LANDINGS

Parachutes help **skydivers** land safely after jumping out of planes. But can they help your toys float to the ground too? Yes, they can! With just a few supplies, you can make your own toy parachute. Happy landings!

WHAT YOU NEED

- square paper napkin
- duct tape
- paper punch
- scissors
- string
- small toy figure

7

WHAT YOU DO

STEP 1

Unfold the napkin and spread it out flat.

Wrap a strip of duct tape around the front and back of each corner of the napkin.

STEP 2

Use a paper punch to make a hole in each taped corner of the napkin.

11

STEP 3

Cut a piece of string that is equal in length to the width of the napkin.

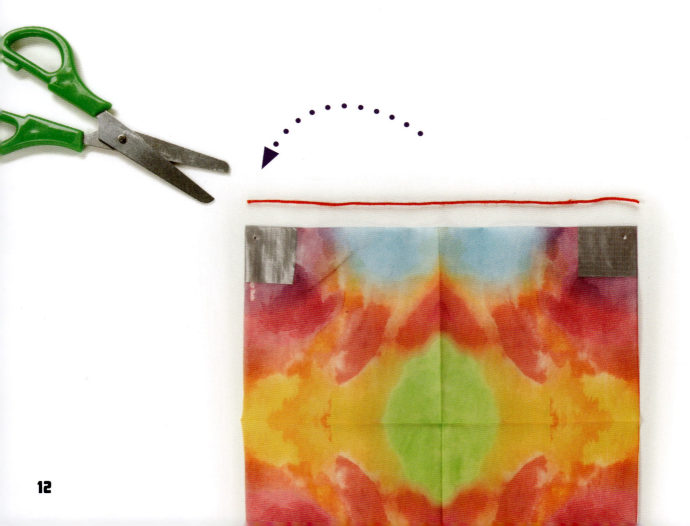

Repeat this step with three more pieces of string.

STEP 4

Thread one piece of string through the hole in one corner of the napkin. Tie the end of the string into a knot to fasten it to the corner.

Repeat this step with the remaining strings and the other corners of the napkin.

STEP 5

Tie the loose ends of two strings around one of the toy figure's arms.

Tie the remaining two strings around the toy figure's other arm.

STEP 6

Throw the toy figure and its parachute into the air.

Watch as the parachute opens, and the toy figure floats to the ground!

TAKE IT FURTHER

Try making a parachute that will work for larger action figures or stuffies. Instead of using a paper napkin, cut a larger square out of a plastic bag.

Test your bigger parachute on different sized toys. Which toys float to the ground faster or slower than others?

BEHIND THE SCIENCE

Gravity pulls a skydiver toward the ground. When the parachute opens, it increases the skydiver's **air resistance**. This strong upward **force** pushes against gravity's downward pull. As a result, the skydiver slows down to a speed that's safer for landing.

GLOSSARY

air resistance (AIR ri-ZISS-tuhnss)—the force of air rubbing against things

force (FORS)—any action that changes the movement of an object

gravity (GRAV-uh-tee)—a force that pulls objects with mass together; gravity pulls objects down toward the center of earth

skydiver (SKYE-dye-vuhr)—a person with a parachute who jumps from an airplane

ABOUT THE AUTHOR

Christopher Harbo is a children's book editor from Minnesota who loves reading and writing. During his career, he has helped publish countless fiction and nonfiction books—and has even written a few too. His favorite nonfiction topics include science and history. His favorite fiction books feature superheroes, adventurers, and space aliens.